# LIVING THINGS

## By • ADRIENNE • MASON

### PHOTOGRAPHS BY RAY BOUDREAU

KIDS CAN PRESS

First U.S. edition 1998
Text copyright © 1997 by Adrienne Mason
Photographs copyright © 1997 by Ray Boudreau

Neither the Publisher nor the Author shall be liable for any damage
which may be caused or sustained as a result of conducting any of the
activities in this book without specifically following instructions,
conducting the activities without proper supervision or ignoring the
cautions contained in the text.

Published in Canada by
Kids Can Press Ltd.
29 Birch Avenue
Toronto, ON M4V 1E2

Published in the U.S. by
Kids Can Press Ltd.
85 River Rock Drive, Suite 202
Buffalo, NY 14207

Edited by Valerie Wyatt
Designed by James Ireland

Printed in Hong Kong by Wing King Tong
Company Limited

CMC    97 0 9 8 7 6 5 4 3 2
CM PA  98 0 9 8 7 6 5 4 3 2

**Canadian Cataloguing in Publication Data**

Mason, Adrienne
    Living things

(Starting with science)
Includes index.

ISBN 1-55074-343-0 (bound)   ISBN 1-55074-393-7 (pbk.)

1. Biology — Experiments — Juvenile literature.
2. Biology — Juvenile literature.  I. Boudreau, Ray.  II. Title.
III. Series.

QH316.5.M37 1997          j570'.078          C96-931707-7

Kids Can Press is a Nelvana company

# Table of contents

# Is it alive?

Living things are all around you. They can be plants, animals, fungi or tiny bacteria, but they all have some things in common:

• Living things are made of cells. Cells are like engines that operate living things. The cells in your body help you blink, breathe, grow, move and much more.

• Living things need food, air, water and a habitat (a place to live).

• Living things grow, reproduce and respond to the environment around them.

There are seven living things on this page. Can you find them?

# Worm farm

All living things need food to live and grow. Start a worm farm and watch what happens when some worms get eating.

## You will need:
- potting or garden soil
- a large, wide-mouthed jar
- a water mister
- sand
- apple and carrot peelings
- 4 earthworms (look for them on the sidewalk or in a garden after a rain)
- black construction paper and tape

## What to do:
**1.** Put a layer of soil 2.5 cm (1 inch) deep in the bottom of the jar. Use the mister to moisten the soil. Add a 2.5-cm (1-inch) layer of sand. Repeat layers until you are 5 cm (2 inches) from the top of the jar. Fill the rest of the jar with peelings.

**2.** Put the worms on top of the peelings.

**3.** Tape the construction paper around the outside of the jar and put the jar in a dark place. Don't disturb the jar for a week, except to add more peelings and a light sprinkling of water once during the week.

**4.** After a week, carefully remove the construction paper. Can you see the worm trails? When you are finished observing, empty your worm farm into the soil outside.

## What's happening?
The earthworms act like nature's composters. The peelings and other food they eat are broken down and pass through their digestive system. Then the bits of food are deposited in the soil as "castings." The castings help enrich the soil so that plants will grow more.

### Living things need food
All living things need food to give them energy for growth and repair. Living things get food in different ways. Animals must find plants or other animals to eat. Plants make their own food.

# Tattoo a plant

Plants can't eat, so they need to make their own food. How do plants do this? Grow a plant and find out.

## You will need:
- scissors
- cardboard
- 3 paper clips
- a young plant

## What to do:
**1.** Cut the first letter of your name or any other shape out of the cardboard. This is your tattoo. Cut out three tattoos.

**2.** Paper clip a tattoo to the upper surface of the leaves of the plant — one tattoo per leaf.

**3.** Put the plant in a sunny spot and water it every other day.

**4.** After a week, remove the tattoos. What do the leaves look like? Wait a week. Now how do the leaves look?

## What's happening?
The plant's leaves are like mini-factories. They make food using light, water, a gas called carbon dioxide, and chlorophyll, the chemical that makes leaves green. This process is called photosynthesis. When you covered part of a leaf with the tattoo, light couldn't reach the leaf, so food stopped being made in that part of the leaf. What do you think would happen if you covered the whole leaf?

# Feed a fungus

To make bread, you need a living thing — a fungus called yeast. Like all living things, yeast needs to eat. But what?

## You will need:

- 3 small drinking glasses, each with 125 mL (½ cup) warm water
- 15 mL (1 tablespoon) sugar
- 15 mL (1 tablespoon) salt
- 45 mL (3 tablespoons) baking yeast

## What to do:

**1.** Stir the sugar into one glass of water and the salt into another.
**2.** Sprinkle 15 mL (1 tablespoon) yeast into each of the three glasses and stir.
**3.** Put the glasses in a warm place and watch them for 5 minutes. Which glass has the most foamy bubbles?

## What's happening?

When yeast finds food it likes, it produces bubbles of carbon dioxide gas. The more bubbles, the better it likes the food. Which food did your yeast prefer? During bread baking, the bubbles will burst and leave holes.

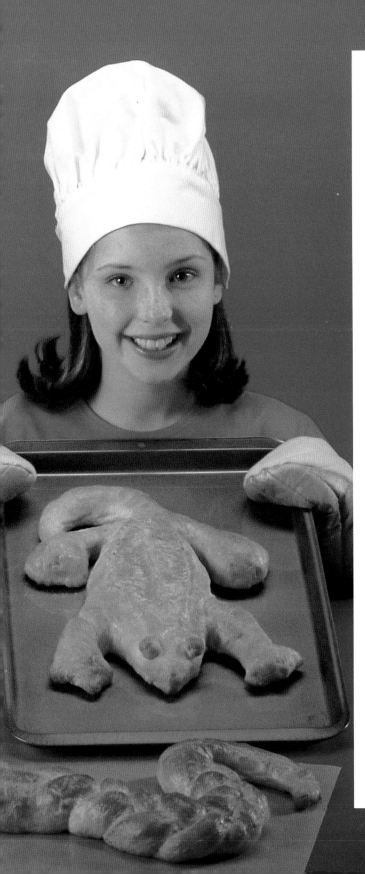

## BAKE BREAD

Use yeast to bake some bread.

### You will need:

- 500 mL (2 cups) very warm water
- 15 mL (1 tablespoon) each of sugar, yeast, vegetable oil and salt
- 1.25 L (5 cups) white flour

### What to do:

**1.** Pour the warm water into a bowl. Stir in the sugar then sprinkle the yeast on top. Put the bowl in a warm place for 10 minutes. The yeast should bubble.

**2.** Stir in the oil and salt and slowly add the flour. Use your hands, if you wish.

**3.** On a floured counter, punch and fold the dough for 10 minutes — until it's smooth. Add more flour if it's too sticky.

**4.** Put the dough into a clean, oiled bowl. Cover with a clean tea towel and place somewhere warm until the dough has doubled in size — about 2 hours.

**5.** Roll the dough out on a floured counter to 2.5 cm (1 inch) thick. Make the dough into any shape you wish.

**6.** Put your bread on a baking sheet and ask an adult to put it in a 120°C (350°F) oven for about 30 minutes.

# What's your lung level?

Breathe in. Now breathe out. You need air to live and grow. Other living things need air, too. How much air do you need? Here's how to find out.

## You will need:
- a 4-L (4-quart) plastic milk jug
- a piece of rubber tubing 0.5 m (2 feet) long (available at hardware stores)
- a measuring cup

## What to do:
1. Fill the milk jug full of water.
2. Half fill a sink or large bowl with water.
3. Cover the opening of the jug with your hand. Turn the jug upside down and put the opening down into the water. Remove your hand.
4. Ask a friend to hold the jug. Put one end of the tubing into the jug.
5. Breathe in, then blow into the tubing. Blow out as much air as you can.
6. Remove the tubing. Cover the opening of the jug with your hand. Lift the jug out of the water and turn it right side up.
7. Use the measuring cup to fill up the jug. How much water did you add? This is how much air you breathed out.

## What's happening?
You blow air into the jug and water out. How much air you can blow in depends on the size and strength of your lungs. Ask some friends and adults to try the same test and see how they do.

## Living things need air
When animals breathe, they exchange new air for used air. Breathing in brings oxygen to the blood. The body needs oxygen to operate. Breathing out gets rid of carbon dioxide, a waste gas that is no longer needed. Even plants "breathe." Gases move in and out through tiny openings on their leaves.

# Egg heads

You are full of water — it is in your blood, in your cells, even in your bones. All living things need water. But how much? Grow some tasty sprouts to find out.

## You will need:
- a small nail
- 3 eggs
- a bowl
- 3 cotton balls
- some alfalfa seeds (available in the bulk food section of grocery stores)

## What to do:
**1.** Using the nail, carefully make a hole about the size of a quarter in one end of each egg.

**2.** Hold the eggs over the bowl and let the insides drain out. (Use the insides for cooking.)

**3.** Put a cotton ball into each egg shell.

**4.** Sprinkle enough seeds on each cotton ball to cover it.

**5.** Add just enough water to one egg shell to moisten the cotton ball thoroughly. Fill the second egg shell with water so that the cotton and seeds are completely covered. Do not water the third egg shell.

**6.** Put the egg shells in a sunny place. Over the next week, keep the cotton ball moist in the first one and the seeds covered with water in the second one. Which egg head grows the best sprout "hair"?

## What's happening?
Like all living things, seeds need water to grow. The outer coating on the seed softens, and the roots, stems and leaves begin to grow from it. But seeds can have too much water. In the egg with the most water, the seeds couldn't get any air, so they didn't grow. In the picture on the right, which egg head do you think got just the right amount of water?

## Living things need water

The cells that living things are made of need just the right amount of water to work properly. Without water, living things will die.

# Soda-bottle habitat

Imagine what special gear you would need if you lived in the ocean. Water is not our natural home. Humans live on land, surrounded by air. All living things have a habitat, a place where they prefer to live. What kind of habitat does a sow bug prefer?

## You will need:

- a 2-L (2-quart) plastic soda bottle with cap
- scissors
- damp soil
- some large leaves
- 6 sow bugs or pill bugs

*You can find sow bugs under rocks outside.*

## What to do:

**1.** Ask an adult to cut a flap in the bottle as shown.
**2.** Add damp soil to the bottle until it is half full.

16

**3.** Put the leaves on top of the soil on one side of the bottle.

**4.** Add the sow bugs to the bottle. Close the flap and place the soda bottle in a bright place.

**5**. Wait 20 minutes, then count the sow bugs on each side of the bottle.

## What's happening?

Did most sow bugs like the side with the leaf or the side without? They probably chose the leaf side, because it is dark and shady like their usual habitat. Now that you know what your sow bugs prefer, turn the whole soda bottle into a sow bug habitat. When you are finished observing your sow bugs, empty the soda bottle outside.

## Living things need a habitat

Different kinds of living things prefer different habitats. For example, fish live in water, and earthworms live in the soil. Some plants prefer the sun, others grow well in the shade. The world is full of different habitats.

# The eating game

Take a look at yourself in a mirror. Do you have the same kind of mouth as a frog or hummingbird has? Why not? Try this game with some friends and see.

## You will need:
- a handful each of rice, elastic bands, marbles, cereal, dried pasta, candies
- some kitchen tools such as a clothespin, spoon, skewer, plastic fork (with the center tines removed) or tongs
- a small plastic bag for each player
- a watch with a second hand

## What to do:
**1.** Give each player a clothespin, spoon, tongs, toothpick or other tool. These are your "mouths."
**2.** Put the rice, elastic bands, marbles and other objects in separate piles on a table. This is your "food."
**3.** Give one plastic bag to each player. This is your "stomach."

**4.** The object of the game is to use your "mouth" to put as much "food" as possible into your "stomach." Each player gets 30 seconds to collect food.

## What's happening?
Did some "mouths" work better for certain foods than others? Animals have different mouths because they eat different foods. A frog needs a fast-moving, sticky tongue to snatch insects out of the air. A hummingbird uses its beak like a straw to sip nectar from flowers. You have strong teeth and jaws to bite and chew plants and meat.

## Living things are adapted to their environment
Plant and animal bodies are adapted to the foods they eat and the places they live. Look at birds' feet, for example. Why do you think some birds have claws while others have webbed feet? Plants are adapted, too. For example, desert plants can store water to survive long, dry spells.

# Dirt dwellers

Who lives in the soil? Make this creature-catcher and find out.

## You will need:

- a large, wide-mouthed jar
- a funnel
- a small piece of mesh (cut from a plastic pot scrubber)
- soil from a yard or park
- a lamp
- paper towel
- a magnifying glass (if you have one)

## What to do:

**1.** Set the funnel in the mouth of the jar and cover the opening to the narrow neck of the funnel with the mesh.

**2.** Fill the funnel with soil.

**3.** Shine the light onto the soil. Turn out all the other lights in the room and leave the lamp on overnight.

**4.** In the morning, remove the funnel and empty the jar onto a paper towel. Look at the creatures — use a magnifying glass, if you have one. Are all the creatures the same?

## What's happening?

Most soil animals prefer moist, dark places. They burrow down through the soil to escape the heat and light of the lamp and fall into the jar. Return the animals to the soil outside when you are done.

### There is variety in living things

How many different types of creatures did you find? Living things come in all shapes, sizes and colors. Variety is important in nature. For example, what if all living things ate the same food? Would there be enough food to go around?

# Fingerprint detective

Here's a mystery. What do you have that no one else does? Become a detective and find out.

## You will need:

- a soft (number 2) lead pencil
- scrap paper
- clear adhesive tape
- white paper
- a magnifying glass (if you have one)

## What to do:

**1.** Scribble on the scrap paper to make a very dark spot of pencil lead.

**2.** Rub your pointer finger in the lead.

**3.** Stick a small piece of tape across the pencil smudge on your finger, then gently peel off the tape. Your fingerprint will come off with it.

**4.** Stick the tape to a piece of white paper.

**5.** Take a close look at your fingerprint with a magnifying glass.

**6.** Take fingerprints from your friends and family. Compare their prints with yours.

## What's happening?

Nobody else has fingerprints exactly like yours — not even if you are an identical twin. There are always slight differences in living things. Some of these differences can be important. For example, a hawk with sharp eyesight has a better chance of finding food than one with weak eyesight.

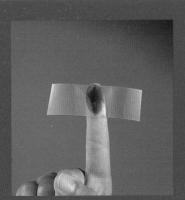

# Life cycles

You grow bigger as you grow older, but some living things change completely. This is called "metamorphosis." Try raising some mealworms and watch them go through metamorphosis. Note: A complete mealworm metamorphosis may take up to six weeks.

## You will need:
- a clear glass or plastic container
- bran
- potato or apple wedges
- 6 mealworms (available at pet shops)
- paper towels

## What to do:
**1.** Half fill the container with bran. Set potato or apple wedges on top and sprinkle on the mealworms.

**2.** Check the mealworms every few days and replace the apple or potato if they dry up or go moldy. Also add more bran if necessary.

**3.** Twice a week, gently dump the bran out onto a paper towel and take a look. Can you find the three stages of the mealworm's metamorphosis shown on page 25? (The fourth stage — the egg — is too small to see.)

## What's happening?
A mealworm goes through a four-stage metamorphosis in its life cycle. It changes from **larva** (worm) to **pupa** to adult **beetle**, which lays the **eggs** that hatch into new larvae. Birth, growth, reproduction and death make up the life cycle of living things.

## Metamorphosis
Some other animals, including frogs and butterflies, go through metamorphosis, too. Why do they change their shape? Having two forms means they can eat different foods and live in different habitats at different times during their life cycle. So they do not depend on just one food or habitat.

larva (worm) stage

pupa stage

adult beetle stage

# Flower power

Flowers come in all shapes and sizes. Here's how to make a simple flower press and start a flower collection.

## You will need:
- a hole punch
- 2 pieces of cardboard 15 cm x 15 cm (6 inches x 6 inches) square
- 2 shoelaces
- flowers (use flowers from a garden or a store, not wild flowers)
- paper towels
- a heavy book

## What to do:
**1.** Punch holes in the corners of both pieces of cardboard.
**2.** Lace the shoelaces through the holes as shown.

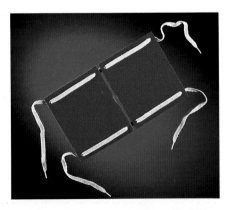

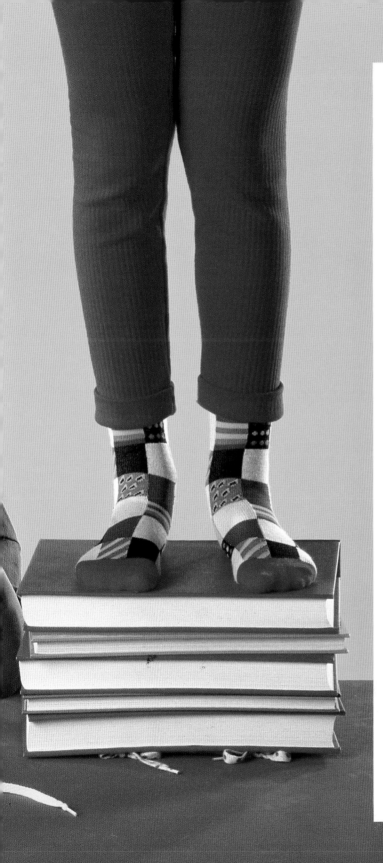

**3.** Place your flowers between two paper towels and put them into your plant press.

**4.** Tightly tie the edges of your press together and put the press under the heavy book.

**5.** After four days, carefully remove the pressed flowers and display your collection. How many different shapes and colors of flowers did you find?

## What's happening?

Pretty shapes and colors are two ways flowers attract insects. Scent is another. Why do flowers need to attract insects? Insects carry pollen from the male part of the flower in one plant to the female part in another plant so that seeds can form and grow into new plants.

### Living things reproduce

All living things eventually die. To keep their species alive, they must create new living things. Plants produce seeds, chickens lay eggs, dogs have puppies, and your parents had you. This is called reproduction.

# Secret smells

How do you communicate? With your voice? Your eyes? Body language? How about with smell? Many plants — and even some animals — use smell to communicate. Can you pick up a scent signal?

## You will need:

- cotton balls
- vanilla extract (or other liquid with a strong smell)
- 5 empty film canisters (or other small containers)
- a blindfold

## What to do:

**1.** Soak the cotton balls in vanilla extract and place some in each film canister.
**2.** In a safe place in your home or yard, set out a scent trail for a friend. Put the film canisters containing the cotton balls about 1 m (1 yard) apart to make a trail.
**3.** Blindfold your friend and see if she can follow the trail just by sniffing.
**4.** Trade places. Have your friend set out the scent trail, and you try to follow it.

## Living things communicate

Many insects, such as ants, communicate with one another using scent trails. Other living things use colors and patterns, sounds or body language to communicate. These signals warn of danger or anger or help living things find a mate.

# For parents and teachers

*The activities in this book are designed to teach children about the characteristics and basic needs of living things. Some experiments explore living things' requirements for food, air, water and a habitat. Other activities introduce the concepts of growth, reproduction, adaptation and communication. Here are some ideas to extend the activities in this book.*

## Is it alive?

Look around you for objects that have been made from living things. Many everyday items are made from materials that were once alive, such as paper, wood, wool, cotton, silk, cork and rayon.

## Worm farm

Bacteria and fungi also decompose, or rot, the peelings and help return nutrients to the soil. To see what bacteria and fungi do, set up a worm farm minus the worms. At the end of one week, examine the peelings.

## Tattoo a plant

To see the other pigments, besides green, in leaves, tear some leaves into small pieces, place them in a jar and cover with rubbing alcohol. After five minutes dip one end of a strip of paper coffee filter into the solution. When the strip is completely wet, remove it and let dry.

## Feed a fungus

Mold is another type of fungus. To observe molds, leave slices of different foods on a kitchen counter for an hour, then place them in separate plastic bags and seal. Put the bags in a dark cupboard and observe every few days. Do not open the bags.

## What's your lung level?

Plants take in gases to help make food during photosynthesis and release waste gases back into the air. The gases pass through openings called stoma on the leaves. Cover the underside of one plant leaf with petroleum jelly and watch what happens over several days.

## Egg heads

How much water do living things contain? Cut slices of different fruits and vegetables. The longer they take to dry, the more water they contain.

## Soda-bottle habitat

Plants have habitats, too. Look for different plants in shady, sunny, wet and dry habitats in a backyard or park.

## The eating game

Observe birds in the wild, in a zoo or in pictures, and compare their beaks to kitchen utensils and other tools.

## Dirt dwellers

Gather dirt samples from a variety of habitats — gardens, forests and fields, for example. Compare the variety of animals found in the different habitats.

## Fingerprint detective

Look for other traits that are genetically controlled. See who can roll their tongue, spread their toes, wiggle their small toe sideways, or flare their nostrils. Can all of the members of a family do the same things?

## Life cycles

Collect a caterpillar and place it in a jar with the plants it was eating. Put air holes in the lid. Monitor the caterpillar as it changes into a pupa and then an adult moth or butterfly. As soon as it hatches into an adult, release it outdoors.

## Flower power and Secret smells

In a garden, follow an insect. Which flowers does it prefer? Do certain insects prefer particular colors, shapes or smells?

Animals sometimes use body language to communicate. Try using your body to say: danger!, come here, stay away, and other messages.

# Words to know

**bacteria:** simple, one-celled organisms that can break down (rot) animal or vegetable material

**chlorophyll:** the chemical in plants that makes leaves green. It is needed for photosynthesis.

**digestive system:** the parts of an animal's body where food is broken down and passed on to other parts of the body

**fungi:** a group of living things that are neither plants nor animals. Mold, fungus, mushrooms and yeast are types of fungi.

**metamorphosis:** a process that some animals undergo as they grow from egg to adult. It involves several changes to their body form.

**mold:** a kind of fungus that grows on food, rotting plants and animals

**photosynthesis:** the process by which green plants make their own food, using carbon dioxide (a gas in the air), light and water

**reproduction:** the process by which living things create new life

**seeds:** tiny baby plants protected by a covering

# Index